This Notebook Belongs To